THIS BOOK BELONGS TO

....

HI THERE!

ARE YOU READY TO GET MAKING? OF COURSE YOU ARE!

THIS CRAFT BOOK IS JAM-PACKED WITH RECYCLABLE ARTSY PROJECTS AND SIMPLE STEP-BY-STEP GUIDES. YOU'LL FIND OUT HOW TO TURN ALL SORTS OF HOUSEHOLD SCRAPS INTO UNICORNS, SHARKS, PIRATES, AND SO MUCH MORE!

IF YOU WANT, YOU CAN USE OUR HANDY CUTOUT PIECES AT THE BACK OF YOUR BOOK TO HELP YOU WITH YOUR CRAFTS.

SARA STANFORD

WELBECK

Published in 2022 by Welbeck Children's Books
An imprint of Welbeck Children's Limited,
part of Welbeck Publishing Group.
Based in London and Sydney.
www.welbeckpublishing.com

First published in 2018 by Carlton Books Limited as:
I am not a Toilet Roll; I am not a Cereal Box;
I am not an Old Sock; I am not an Eggbox

Text and design copyright © Welbeck Children's Limited 2018

Author: Sara Stanford
Written, designed, illustrated and packaged by: Dynamo Limited
Designer: Sam James
Editor: Jenni Lazell

ISBN: 978-1-78312-909-6

Printed in Dongguan, China
10 9 8 7 6 5 4 3 2 1

YOU WILL NEED

- TAPE
- GLUE
- COLORED PAPER
- COLORED CARDSTOCK
- PAINTS
- PAINTBRUSHES
- SAFETY SCISSORS
- STRING

- ALUMINUM FOIL
- PENS
- PENCILS
- BOTTLE CAPS
- BUTTONS
- YARN
- PIPE CLEANERS
- TISSUE PAPER

- STRAWS
- GOOGLY EYES
- GLITTER
- THREAD
- RIBBON
- CRAFT STICKS
- ABSORBENT COTTON

- LOTS OF TOILET PAPER ROLLS, CEREAL BOXES, EGG CARTONS, AND A FEW OLD SOCKS
- UNCOOKED RICE—FOR FILLING YOUR SOCK CREATIONS
- SCRAPS OF MATERIAL, FABRIC, SOCKS, AND COTTON BATTING FOR STUFFING

YOU'LL NEED A GROWN-UP TO HELP YOU WITH ALL OF THE MAKES!

CONTENTS

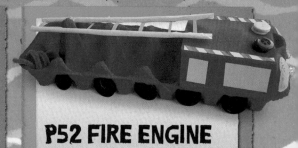

SHAAAAARK!

I'M A **TERRIFYING** SHARK HERE TO **CHOMP** ON UNSUSPECTING **TOES** IN THE **BATHTUB!** I DEFINITELY WOULDN'T TURN TO TOILET ROLL MUSH UNDERWATER...

WATCH OUT!!

YOU WILL NEED

- ONE EMPTY TOILET PAPER ROLL
- BLUE AND WHITE PAINT
- PAINTBRUSH AND PEN
- SAFETY SCISSORS
- BLUE AND WHITE CARDSTOCK
- A BOWL (TO DRAW AROUND)
- TAPE
- GOOGLY EYES

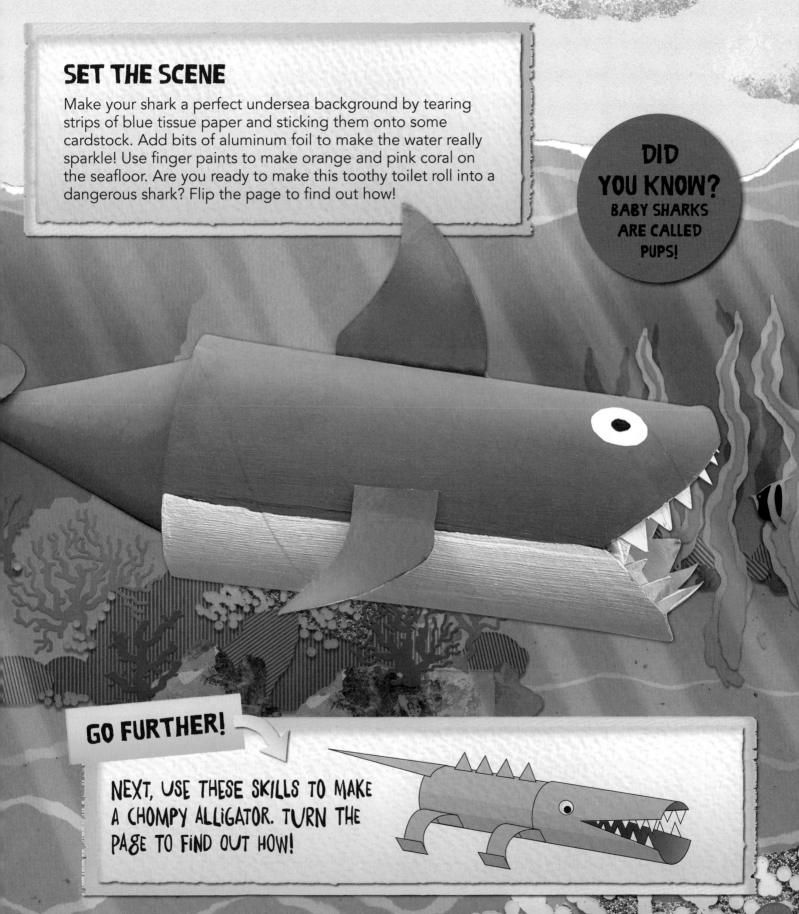

SET THE SCENE

Make your shark a perfect undersea background by tearing strips of blue tissue paper and sticking them onto some cardstock. Add bits of aluminum foil to make the water really sparkle! Use finger paints to make orange and pink coral on the seafloor. Are you ready to make this toothy toilet roll into a dangerous shark? Flip the page to find out how!

DID YOU KNOW? BABY SHARKS ARE CALLED PUPS!

GO FURTHER!

NEXT, USE THESE SKILLS TO MAKE A CHOMPY ALLIGATOR. TURN THE PAGE TO FIND OUT HOW!

I AM NOT A TOILET PAPER ROLL...

I'M A SHARK!

1 Paint your toilet paper roll so that one half is white and the other half is blue. When the paint is completely dry, snip two triangles out of the end of the toilet roll to make the shark's mouth.

2 To make the tail, draw a circle on the blue cardstock by drawing around a bowl (a cereal bowl would be perfect). Then carefully cut a large triangle out of the circle, just like the above picture.

3 Roll the two sides of your blue circle together to make a cone and tape it in place. Slot the cone into the end of the toilet paper roll and tape it together.

4 Add extra details by cutting these tail and fin shapes from your blue cardstock, then tape them on.

5

Create a set of pointed teeth by cutting zigzags out of two strips of white cardstock. Attach them along the top and bottom of the shark's mouth.

6

Complete your fearsome shark by adding some googly eyes from the back of your book.

I AM NOT A TOILET PAPER ROLL...
I'M AN ALLIGATOR!

This time, paint two toilet paper rolls green and tape them together to make the body. Snip in a mouth shape, just like last time, and add your spiked teeth. Then, cut a pointed tail and feet from green cardstock and attach googly eyes. Finally, cut out green triangles of cardstock and attach these to the alligator's back!

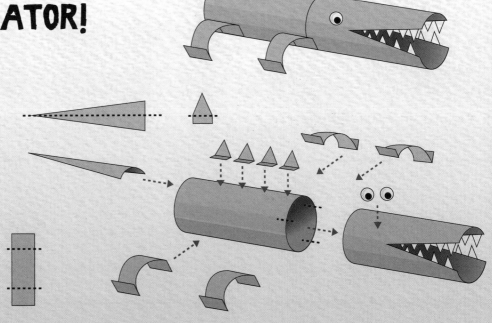

SET THE SCENE

Create a background for your bat using night-time colors—dark blue or black work best! Paint a shiny moon and stars in yellow, or cut them out using aluminum foil and glue them down. Add a sprinkle of glitter for shooting stars, too. Turn the page to find out how to make your very own bat-tastic buddy in six easy steps!

IT'S SO COMFY SNOOZING UPSIDE DOWN. ZZZZ!

DID YOU KNOW?
THERE ARE OVER 1,000 DIFFERENT TYPES OF BAT SPECIES ON THE PLANET!

GO FURTHER!

BESIDES A BAT, YOU CAN ALSO MAKE A FOX OR PEACOCK USING THIS TECHNIQUE. JUST TURN THE PAGE AND WE'LL SHOW YOU HOW.

I'M A BAT!

1

Fold the ends of your toilet paper roll toward each other to give your bat some ears. Now do the same to the bottom of your toilet paper roll to make the bat's feet. Tape the shape in place if needed.

2

Paint your toilet paper roll your battiest black all over, then let it dry while you do Step 3.

3

To make your bat's wings, carefully cut a big "m" shape into black cardstock. Snip some points along the bottom edge like the picture above.

4

When your painted toilet paper roll is dry, use a dab of glue to attach it to the middle of your wings.

5

Take a pair of googly eyes and place them toward the top of your toilet paper roll, under the ears.

6

Finally, give your bat some spooky fangs by cutting two small triangles out of white cardstock. Attach them and your bat is ready to take flight!

I AM NOT A TOILET PAPER ROLL...
I'M A FOX!

To make your fox, paint a toilet paper roll orange and only fold over the top of the toilet roll, not the bottom. Then replace the bat wings with a bushy tail shape cut out from cardstock and tape it to the back of the fox's body. For the face, snip out a white heart-shape, then add googly eyes and black whiskers.

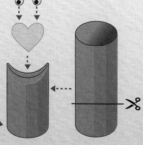

I AM NOT A TOILET PAPER ROLL...
I'M A PEACOCK!

If you can make a fox, then you can make a peacock! Look at the diagram and you will see that the same teardrop shape that is used for the fox tail can be used for pea-cock feathers. Also use the heart shape, but on its tummy this time!

ELEPHANT!

WITH MY HUGE FEET AND A "TOOT" OF MY TRUNK, I MAKE QUITE A RACKET. NO TOILET PAPER ROLL COULD EVER BE AS NOISY AS ME!

STOMP, STOMP, STOMP!

YOU WILL NEED

- ONE EMPTY TOILET PAPER ROLL
- WHITE, BLACK, AND GRAY PAINT
- PAINTBRUSH
- BLACK PEN OR PENCIL
- GLUE
- GOOGLY EYES

SET THE SCENE

Make a jungle scene for your elephant pal by layering different shades of green. You could even try making tree trunks from paper towel rolls painted brown. Flip the page to see how to make a rumble in the jungle by turning your toilet paper roll into a mighty elephant!

Flip the page to see how to make a rumble in the jungle by turning your toilet paper roll into a mighty elephant!

DID YOU KNOW?
ELEPHANTS ARE THE LARGEST LAND MAMMAL, AND THEY LIVE TOGETHER IN GROUPS LED BY THE OLDEST FEMALE.

TRUMPETY TRUMP!

GO FURTHER!

YOU CAN MAKE AN EIGHT-LEGGED OCTOPUS PAL FROM A TOILET PAPER ROLL, TOO! WE'LL SHOW YOU EXACTLY WHAT TO DO ON THE NEXT PAGE.

I AM NOT A TOILET PAPER ROLL...
I'M AN ELEPHANT!

1

For the trunk, make two cuts from the bottom of the toilet paper roll until you reach about halfway up.

2

Carefully cut big ear shapes on each side of your toilet paper roll (be sure to leave enough room for the elephant's face in the middle). Then fold the ears forward to make them stick out.

3

Cut two long, thin triangles on either side of the first cuts you made, leaving two tusk shapes at the top of each one. Now paint your elephant!

4

When the paint is dry, dot toenails on the elephant's feet using the other end of the paintbrush. Add more details with a black pen.

5

Attach some googly eyes from the back of your book to make your elephant come to life!

6

Paint a shadow on the ears of your elephant, using black paint to add a bit of extra detail.

I AM NOT A TOILET ROLL...
I'M AN OCTOPUS!

Do you want to make an octopus instead? Carefully snip the base of your toilet paper roll into eight legs— you should plan to cut about halfway up the toilet paper roll. Then fold down the legs, like this. Finally, paint your octopus in bright colors and let it dry before adding some googly eyes.

ROCKET!

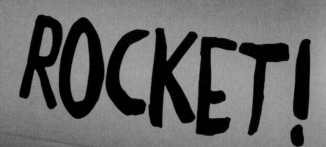

ZOOM! UP, UP, AND AWAY i GO, i AM A ROCKET, DON'T YOU KNOW? JUST LOOK AT ME GO AS I SOAR THROUGH SPACE. THERE'S NO WAY THAT I'VE BEEN MADE FROM TISSUE PAPER AND PAINTS!

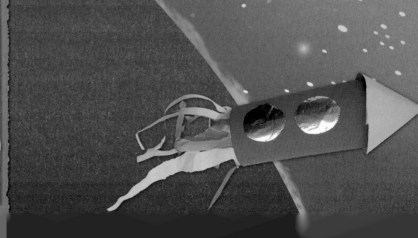

YOU WILL NEED

- ONE TOILET PAPER ROLL
- COLORED PAINT
- COLORED CARDSTOCK
- SAFETY SCISSORS
- TAPE AND GLUE
- ALUMINUM FOIL
- TISSUE PAPER

SET THE SCENE

Decorate a piece of black cardstock with aluminum foil, silver stars, and colorful planets for an out-of-this-world background. Paint planets, copy them from a book, or cut pictures out of a magazine. Want to make your very own awesome rocket? Of course you do! Blast off to the next page to find out how…

DID YOU KNOW? HUMANS FIRST LANDED (AND WALKED!) ON THE MOON IN 1969.

I'M OFF TO VISIT THE MOON…

GO FURTHER!

IF YOU DON'T LIKE MAKING ROCKETS, YOU CAN TRY THESE FANTASTIC FAIRY HOUSES INSTEAD. TURN OVER AND WE'LL SHOW YOU JUST WHAT TO DO.

I AM NOT A TOILET PAPER ROLL...
I'M A ROCKET!

1

Paint your toilet paper roll all over in any color you want (we've gone for rocket red!). Let it dry.

2

Make a circle by drawing around a large roll of tape or a cereal bowl and cut it out. Snip out a large triangle like above and roll it into a cone shape. Use some sticky tape to keep it in place.

3

Tape the cone in place on top of the rocket, then attach some aluminum foil circles to make portholes.

4

Tear fire-colored tissue paper into strips.

Tape the shredded tissue paper to the inside of the rocket at the bottom.

5

Now that you know how, you can make lots of different colouful rockets! Get creative by decorating them in fun ways.

6

I AM NOT A TOILET PAPER ROLL...
I'M A FAIRY HOUSE!

Making fairy houses from toilet paper rolls is almost the same as making rockets. This time, when you make your paper cone, cut to give it a zigzag edge. Next cut out a little door for your fairies to come and go as they please, and make windows from paper or paint them on—it's up to you!

PiRATE!

HELLO THERE, MATEY! I BE A PIRATE, AND I'VE **SAILED THE SEVEN SEAS** ON MY SHIP in search of **TREASURE**. ANYONE WHO SAYS I'M A TOILET PAPER ROLL CAN **WALK THE PLANK!**

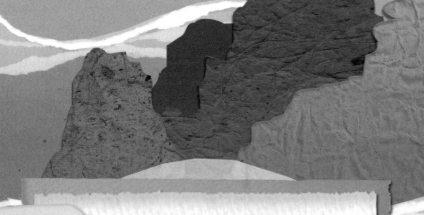

YOU WILL NEED

- ONE EMPTY TOILET PAPER ROLL
- PAINTS AND PAINTBRUSHES
- WHITE PAPER
- SAFETY SCISSORS
- GLUE
- BLACK CARDSTOCK
- BLACK PEN
- OPTIONAL: TISSUE PAPER

SET THE SCENE

Make an island scene for your pirate ship with a sheet of blue paper for the sea and a yellow paper desert island stuck on top. Now you're ready for treasure hunting. X marks the spot! Ready to make your pirate pal? Turn the page to find out how.

ARRR, ME HEARTIES!

DID YOU KNOW?
LOTS OF PIRATE SHIPS HAVE A FLAG WITH A SKULL AND CROSSBONES ON IT. THIS IS CALLED THE JOLLY ROGER.

GO FURTHER!

MAKE A TOILET PAPER ROLL TREASURE CHEST FOR YOUR PIRATES TO KEEP THEIR PRECIOUS TREASURE! TURN THE PAGE TO FOLLOW OUR SIMPLE STEP-BY-STEP GUIDE.

I'M A PIRATE!

1

Paint half of your toilet paper roll in a skin color of your choice and then let it dry.

2

To make a striped top, cut a strip of paper (6 in x 2 in). Now paint or draw some stripes.

3

Stick your top on your pirate, then paint the bottom of the toilet roll black for the trousers.

4

Cut a pirate hat shape out of black cardstock. Then cut out a skull and crossbones from white paper and attach them to the hat.

5

Tape your hat to the top of your toilet paper roll. Draw your pirate's face with a black pen and add an eye patch for the finishing touch. Arrr, me hearties! Ready to set sail!

6

If you prefer, you could make a bandana for your pirate buddy! Just wrap tissue paper around your pirate's head and make a little knot shape on one side.

I AM NOT A TOILET PAPER ROLL...
I'M A TREASURE CHEST!

First, cut a toilet paper roll in half width-wise to make the curved lid of the chest. Then cut a toilet paper roll in half length-wise and flatten out the card. Next make folds in the flattened-out card to tape it into a box. Finally pop the lid inside and paint to decorate your chest.

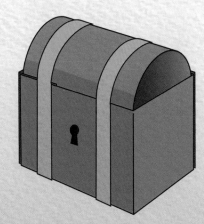

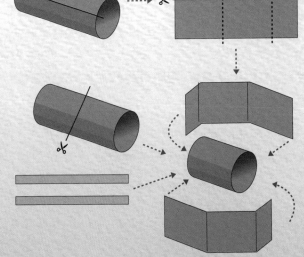

NiNJAAAA!

WATCH ME ROLL WITH MY **AWESOME NINJA SKILLS**. I'M THE SPEEDIEST AND MOST **POWERFUL NINJA** AROUND, SO THERE'S **NO WAY** THAT I AM A TOILET PAPER ROLL.

Hi-YAH!

YOU WILL NEED

- ONE EMPTY TOILET PAPER ROLL
- DARK PAINT
- SAFETY SCISSORS
- PINK PAPER
- BLACK PEN
- GLUE
- BLACK CARDSTOCK
- STRING

SET THE SCENE

Cut out rectangles from tracing paper and attach them to a sheet of black cardstock to make a cool Dojo-style background. Want to give a toilet paper roll some nifty ninja moves? You can make your nimble ninja on the next page.

DID YOU KNOW? NINJAS ORIGINALLY CAME FROM JAPAN AND WERE CALLED SHINOBI-NO-MONO.

I'M A MARTIAL ARTS MASTER!

GO FURTHER!

TAKE YOUR MAKE TO THE NEXT LEVEL BY CREATING A HORSE FOR YOUR NINJA TO RIDE. TURN OVER TO FIND OUT HOW.

I AM NOT A TOILET PAPER ROLL...
I'M A NINJA!

1

Paint a toilet paper roll any color you want (we recommend a dark color) and let it dry.

2

Cut a small rectangle from pink paper and draw some eyes. This will be your ninja's face.

3

Attach the face to the toilet paper roll, then carefully snip some small rectangles out of black cardstock and glue them over your ninja's eyes to make eyebrows.

4

Next, cut out another thin rectangle from black cardstock (4 in) and get your length of string ready.

5

Tie the string around the ninja's waist and slot the card stick inside, like this.

6

Now you can make a whole ninja crew using different colors. Sayonara for now!

I AM NOT A TOILET PAPER ROLL...
I'M A HORSE!

Tape two toilet paper rolls together, like this, to make the horse's head and body. Slot in a circle of card for the horse's nose and give it some nostrils with black paint. Cut out four legs from cardstock and tape them in place, ready to gallop. Make pointed paper ears and add two googly eyes. Absorbend cotton makes a great mane and tail!

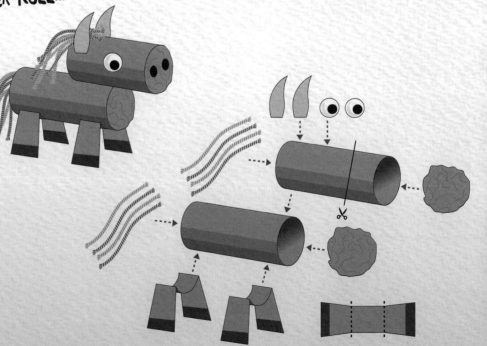

GINGERBREAD MAN!

HELLO THERE! I'M A FRIENDLY GINGERBREAD MAN, SWEET AS CAN BE. MY BUTTONS ARE MADE FROM DELICIOUS CANDY, NOT PAPER AND GLUE.

- ONE EMPTY TOILET PAPER ROLL
- ORANGE PAINT AND PAINTBRUSH
- SAFETY SCISSORS
- ORANGE CARDSTOCK
- STICKY TAPE
- COLORFUL PAPER
- GLUE

SET THE SCENE

Make a cunning fox out of orange and brown paper to help the gingerbread man get across a river of torn blue paper. But watch out for the fox's tricks! Ready to make your toilet paper roll gingerbread man? Turn over to find out how.

DID YOU KNOW? THE BIGGEST GINGERBREAD HOUSE EVER WAS 21 FEET TALL AND MADE IN TEXAS!

I LOVE MY FANCY BOW TIE!

GO FURTHER!

YOU COULD MAKE A SUPER COOL CLOWN USING THIS TECHNIQUE! FIND OUT HOW ON THE NEXT PAGE.

I'M A GINGERBREAD MAN!

1

Paint a toilet paper roll all over with orange or yellow paint and let it dry.

2

Next, cut a balloon shape (as above) out of orange cardstock. Use colored paper or markers to create your gingerbread man's face.

3

Tape the head to the top of the toilet roll.

4

Now, carefully cut two strips of orange cardstock (6 in x 1 in) for the legs, and two strips (6 in x 1/2 in) for the arms.

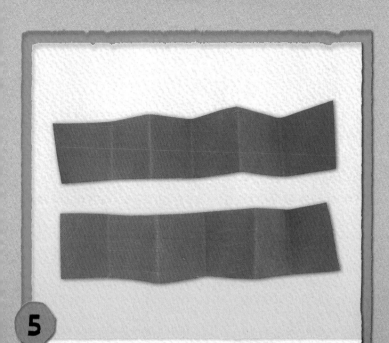

5

Fold the strips of cardstock like this to make them springy. Then use tape to attach the arms and legs to the body.

6

Decorate your new gingerbread buddy by attaching colorful paper buttons and a bright bow tie.

7

Make a simple candy cane by cutting out this shape from cardstock and painting some bright red stripes.

I AM NOT A TOILET PAPER ROLL...

I'M A CLOWN!

Paint your toilet paper roll and then add your colorful bow tie and buttons. This time, you'll need white cardstock for the face! Draw some black crosses for the eyes, then add a red smiley mouth and a round nose. Cut out arms and big feet from cardstock to tape in place and use absorbent cotton to make hair.

CASTLE!

I'M A **BEAUTIFUL** CASTLE! HOME TO THE **FINEST ROYALTY**. WITH MY TALL TOWERS TOPPED WITH **FABULOUS FLAGS**, I'M FAR TOO **GRAND** TO BE MADE FROM CARDSTOCK!

YOU WILL NEED

- THREE EMPTY TOILET PAPER ROLLS
- SAFETY SCISSORS
- PAINTS AND PAINTBRUSHES
- PAPER
- GLUE
- CRAFT STICKS OR TOOTHPICKS
- BLUE AND BROWN PAPER
- BLACK PEN
- TAPE

SET THE SCENE

Pop your castle onto layers of green paper to make the rolling countryside. Add trees like these shown or scrunch up tissue paper for colorful flowers.

Turn over to find out how to transform three toilet paper rolls into a splendid castle fit for a king and queen.

DID YOU KNOW? MOATS PROTECT CASTLES AND KEEP OUT ANY UNWELCOME VISITORS.

GO FURTHER!

WHY STOP AT JUST THREE CASTLE TOWERS? LET'S MAKE YOUR CASTLE EVEN MORE SPECTACULAR! WE'LL SHOW YOU HOW ON THE NEXT PAGE.

I AM NOT A TOILET PAPER ROLL...

I'M A CASTLE!

1

Cut rectangles from the top of your toilet paper roll to create turrets.

2

Repeat Step 1 on two more toilet paper rolls. You could make some towers shorter by trimming the tops off first.

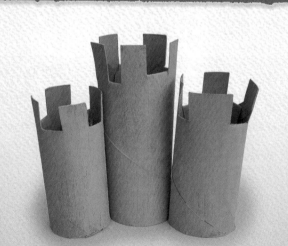

3

Paint all the toilet paper rolls in your favorite color and let them dry.

4

To make flags, cut triangles out of colorful paper and tape them to craft sticks or wooden toothpicks. When your castle is dry, tape the flags to the top of your towers.

5

Cut three windows out of blue paper, and one door out of brown paper or cardstock.

6

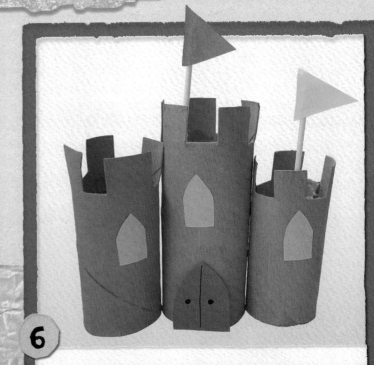

Next, tape all three towers together before attaching your windows and door.

I AM NOT A TOILET PAPER ROLL...
I'M A HUGE CASTLE!

You don't have to stop at just three toilet paper rolls. Keep taping on more and more painted toilet paper roll towers until you make a super grand castle! You could attach all of your towers to a painted cardboard box, like this. Have fun designing lots of different door and window shapes as you go.

MERMAID!

PERCHED ON A ROCK NEAR THE SEASHORE, I SIT AND SING MY MERRY MERMAID SONGS IN THE SUN. WITH MY SHIMMERING TAIL AND LONG HAIR, EVERYONE KNOWS WHO I AM!

TRA LA LA LAAAAAA!

TRA LA LA LAAAA

YOU WILL NEED

- ONE TOILET PAPER ROLL
- PAINTS AND PAINTBRUSHES
- SAFETY SCISSORS
- COLORFUL PAPER
- CARDSTOCK
- GLUE AND TAPE
- PEN

SET THE SCENE

Scrunch up brown paper bags to make a rock for your mermaid to sit on. If you visit the beach, you could even bring back some pebbles or shells for a rockpool scene. Ready to make your mermaid? Swim over to the next page to find out how.

Swim over to the next page to find out how.

DID YOU KNOW? A MALE VERSION OF A MERMAID IS CALLED A MERMAN.

GO FURTHER!

DO YOU WANT TO MAKE SOME COLORFUL CORAL REEFS FOR YOUR MERMAID TO SWIM AROUND AND EXPLORE? WE'LL SHOW YOU HOW ON THE NEXT PAGE.

I'M A MERMAID!

1

Paint the top half of your toilet paper roll in a skin color of your choice and the bottom half in a nice, bright color. Let them dry.

2

Carefully cut a mermaid tail from some cardstock. Paint this card to match the color of the tail part of your toilet paper roll and let it dry.

3

For the hair, cut out strips of colorful paper and roll the ends of each strip around a pencil to make it curl.

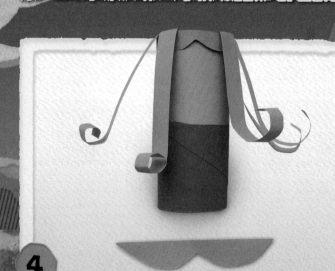

4

Now tape each piece of hair to the top of the toilet paper roll. We attached a paper fringe, too!

5

Make a shell bikini from colorful paper and use a black pen to draw some detail. Now glue the shells in place and draw a smiley face.

6

Tape the tail to the back of your mermaid. Now she's ready for any underwater adventure!

I AM NOT A TOILET PAPER ROLL...
I'M A CORAL REEF!

Paint a toilet paper roll turquoise, and when it's dry, attach strips of colorful paper and tissue to look like coral or seaweed. Then make your own tropical sea creatures and hide them in the bits of coral or seaweed. You can make lots of corals in different colors!

UNICORN!

NO, YOU'RE NOT DREAMING! I AM A MAGICAL UNICORN, AND I'M HERE TO MAKE FRIENDS WITH YOU! GRANTING WISHES AND MAKING YOUR DREAMS COME TRUE IS ALL I'VE EVER WANTED TO DO.

YOU WILL NEED

- ONE EMPTY TOILET PAPER ROLL
- WHITE, PINK, AND BLACK PAINT
- SAFETY SCISSORS
- COLORFUL TISSUE PAPER
- WHITE AND PINK CARDSTOCK
- GLUE AND TAPE
- GLITTER
- RAINBOW TISSUE PAPER
- GOOGLY EYES

JOIN MY UNICORN SQUAD!

SET THE SCENE

Colors at the ready to make a magical rainbow background fit for a unicorn! Attach absorbent cotton on blue cardstock or paper to make fluffy white clouds, then paint or color a beautiful rainbow to light up the sky. Turn the page to make a toilet paper roll's magical unicorn wishes come true.

DID YOU KNOW? UNICORNS ARE MYTHICAL CREATURES, AND LEGEND HAS IT THAT THEY HAVE HEALING POWERS.

GO FURTHER!

ONCE YOU'VE PERFECTED YOUR MAGICAL UNICORN, YOU CAN MAKE THIS FIRE-BREATHING DRAGON TOO. ROAR! FIND OUT HOW ON THE NEXT PAGE.

I AM NOT A TOILET PAPER ROLL...

I'M A UNICORN!

1

Paint your toilet paper roll white with a pink semicircle at the end. When it's dry, dab on two black nostrils using the other end of a paintbrush.

2

Carefully cut out two ear shapes from white cardstock, then cut out smaller ear shapes in pink to make the insides of the ears. Glue them together.

3

To make the unicorn's horn, cut a triangle out of cardstock, roll it into a cone shape, and tape it in place. Next cover the cone in glue and sprinkle with gold glitter until it is completely covered.

4

Carefully tape the horn onto the top of the unicorn. Then add a thick line of glue from the horn to the nose and sprinkle it with glitter.

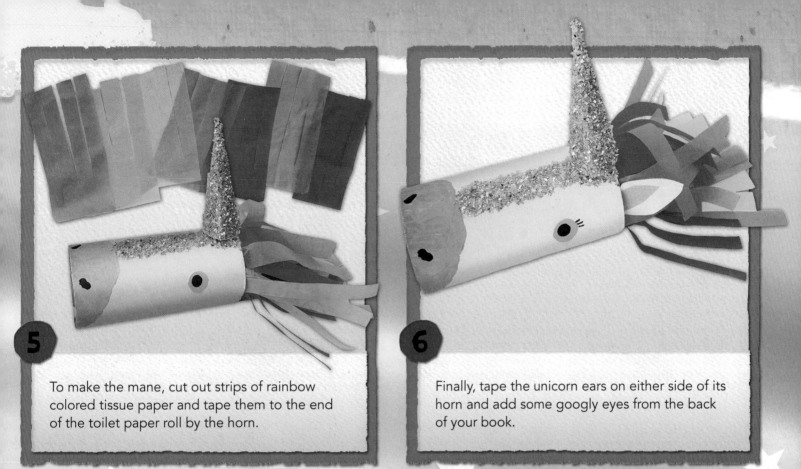

5

To make the mane, cut out strips of rainbow colored tissue paper and tape them to the end of the toilet paper roll by the horn.

6

Finally, tape the unicorn ears on either side of its horn and add some googly eyes from the back of your book.

I AM NOT A TOILET PAPER ROLL...
I'M A DRAGON!

To make your amazing dragon, paint a toilet paper roll red or green and let it dry. For the eyes, attach two googly eyes on pompoms and glue these onto the dragon. Now use two more pompoms for nostrils. Snip strips of yellow and orange tissue paper to tape to the dragon's mouth. ROOAAARR!

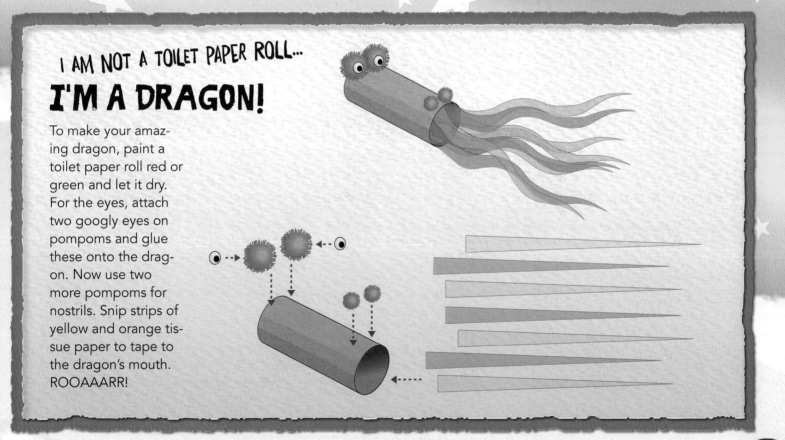

PENGUIN!

I'M YOUR **POCKET**-SIZED PENGUIN PAL, AND I'M **READY** TO PLAY.

LET'S GO FISHING.

MADE FROM AN EGG CARTON - ME? **NO WAY!**

YOU WILL NEED

- ONE EGG CARTON
- SAFETY SCISSORS
- TAPE
- WHITE AND BLACK PAINT
- PAINTBRUSHES
- ORANGE PAPER OR CARDSTOCK
- GLUE
- GOOGLY EYES

SET THE SCENE

You can make a whole waddle of penguins as well as a chilly icescape for them to play on. Scrunch up some tissue paper, then flatten it out a bit and attach it to a piece of cardstock to make a snowy background. Follow the step-by-step guide on the next page to make your frosty friends.

DID YOU KNOW?
A GROUP OF PENGUINS ON LAND IS CALLED A "WADDLE."

EGG CARTONS CAN'T **WADDLE** THROUGH SNOW WITH ORANGE **FLIPPERS** OR GO FISHING IN iCY **WATERS.**

GO FURTHER!

MAKE THESE MiNi MONSTERS USING THE SAME TECHNIQUE. TURN THE PAGE TO FIND OUT HOW!

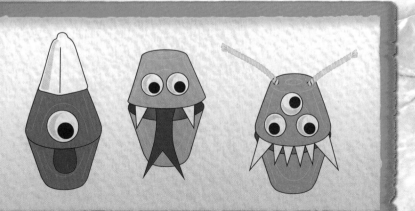

I'M A PENGUIN!

1 To make the body of your penguin pal, carefully cut two egg cups out of an egg carton.

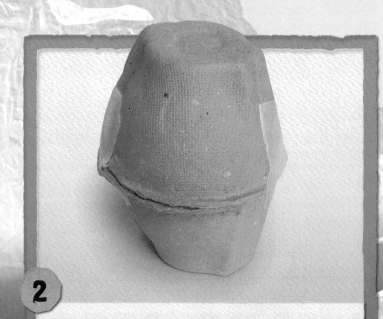

2 Now tape the two egg cups together like this.

3 Paint a white oval to make a tummy for your penguin and then let it dry.

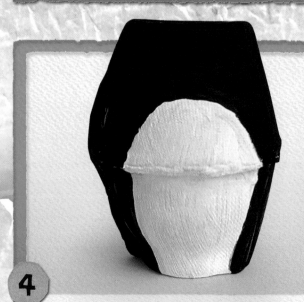

4 Next, paint the rest of your penguin black. Let this dry while you go on to Step 5.

5

Cut out two flat-bottomed ovals and one diamond shape from orange paper. Fold the diamond in half to make a beak.

6

Glue the beak and flippers on your penguin and add some googly eyes from your book!

I AM NOT AN EGG CARTON...

I'M A MINI MONSTER!

Tape two egg carton cups together in the same way as Steps 1 and 2. Paint all over in brightly colored monster shades, then get creative with your monster faces. Cut fangs and tongues out of colored paper and make horns out of pipe cleaners. Finish with some googly eyes.

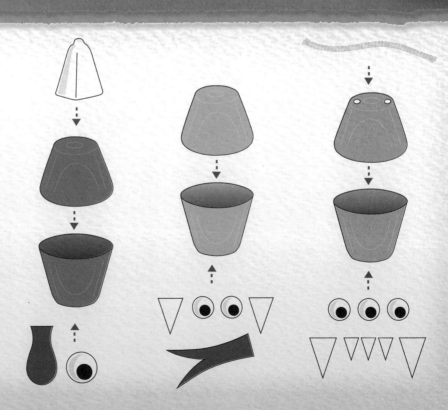

FIRE ENGINE!

WEE-OOH! WHEN THE FIRE ALARM RINGS, I'LL BE THERE IN A FLASH TO **SAVE THE DAY** AND **KEEP** THE CITY **SAFE**.

EGG CARTONS CAN'T BE **HEROES**, SO THAT'S WHY I **MUST** BE A **REAL FIRE ENGINE!**

VROOM!

YOU WILL NEED

- ONE LARGE EGG CARTON
- SAFETY SCISSORS
- RED PAINT
- PAINTBRUSHES
- BLUE PAPER
- GLUE
- TWO STRAWS
- CARDSTOCK
- TAPE
- ONE PIPE CLEANER
- BOTTLE TOPS OR BUTTONS
- ALUMINUM FOIL
- YELLOW PAPER

SET THE SCENE

Create your own city background for your fire engine. Cut lots of different-sized rectangles from colored paper, then line them up across a large sheet of white paper to make your skyline. Now it's time to put your engine to the test. Turn over to start making!

DID YOU KNOW?

THE "JAWS OF LIFE" IS A TOOL ON A FIRE ENGINE THAT RESCUES PEOPLE STUCK IN BUILDINGS OR CARS.

GO FURTHER!

ON THE NEXT PAGE YOU'LL SEE HOW TO MAKE A TERRIFIC TRUCK, AS WELL AS YOUR FIRE ENGINE!

TO THE RESCUE!

I'M A FIRE ENGINE!

1

Carefully cut away part of the egg carton lid like this. Then paint it red and let it dry.

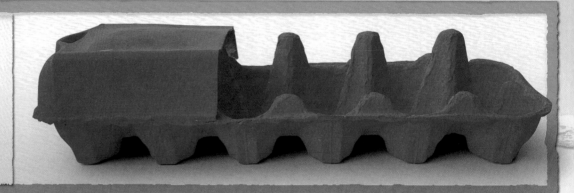

2

Cut two squares and three rectangles out of blue paper to make windows and a windshield, then glue them in place.

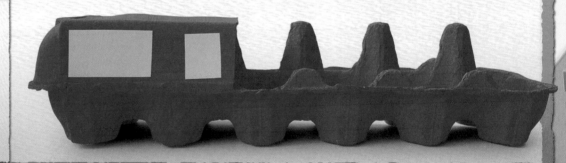

3

Join two straws together by taping small strips of cardstock from one straw to the other. Keep taping more strips of cardstock in the same way until you have a complete ladder.

4

Now, roll a pipe cleaner into a coil to make a firefighter's hose.

5

Add lights by gluing colorful buttons to the top of your engine. Use two small balls of aluminum foil for headlights and glue more buttons to the sides to make the wheels.

6

Paint red stripes on thin strips of yellow paper to decorate your engine. Hooray! You're ready for your first rescue mission.

I AM NOT AN EGG CARTON...
I'M A TRUCK!

To make your truck, cut a smaller egg carton in the same way as the fire engine. Paint it any color you like. You can still add your windows and button wheels, but you don't need to make a ladder or a hose this time. Easy!

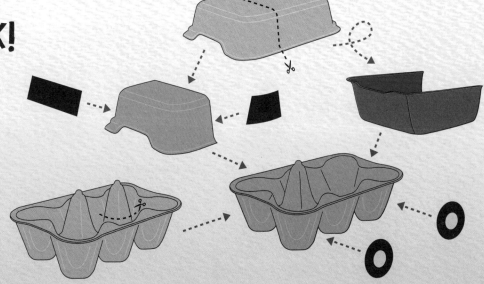

CRAB!

COME AND PLAY WITH ME AT THE BEACH AND SCUTTLE ALONG THE SAND!

WATCH OUT! I HAVE TWO GREAT BIG PINCERS AND PLENTY OF LEGS.

I DON'T CARRY SHELLS; I'VE GOT MY OWN...

YOU WILL NEED

- ONE EGG CARTON
- SAFETY SCISSORS
- ORANGE PAINT
- ORANGE PIPE CLEANERS
- TAPE
- GOOGLY EYES
- PEN

56

SET THE SCENE

Make a crafty rock pool for your egg carton crabs by scrunching up brown paper bags. Place them around a pool made from a blue piece of paper or cardstock. Turn over for a step-by-step guide on how to make your friend.

Turn over for a step-by-step guide on how to make your friend.

DID YOU KNOW?
CRABS HAVE TEN LEGS, AND THIS MAKES THEM DECAPODS.

PINCH!

PINCH!

GO FURTHER!

LOVE CREEPY CRAWLIES? YOU CAN LEARN HOW TO MAKE THESE LITTLE BUGS ON THE NEXT PAGE.

YOU CAN LEARN HOW TO MAKE THESE LITTLE BUGS ON THE NEXT PAGE.

I'M A CRAB!

1

Cut one cup out of your egg carton and paint it bright orange. Let it dry.

2

For each pincer, cut one orange pipe cleaner 4 inches long and bend it in half. Wrap a small piece of pipe cleaner to each end like this.

3

Now tape the pipe cleaners underneath the egg cup so the pincers are at the front of the body.

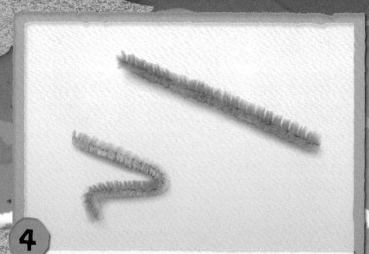

4

Cut eight strips of pipe cleaner about 2 inches long each. Now fold each strip into a curved leg shape.

5

Tape all your legs underneath the egg cup. Make sure there are four on each side.

6

Attach some googly eyes from your book and draw a big smile to finish.

I AM NOT AN EGG CARTON...
I AM A BUG!

Make lots of different creepy crawlies using the same technique! To make a caterpillar, cut out a row of cups from your egg carton, paint them, and thread them together with a pipe cleaner. You could attach the googly eyes to antenna made from pipe cleaners as well. Paint your cups black to make a spider, or red with black spots to make a ladybug.

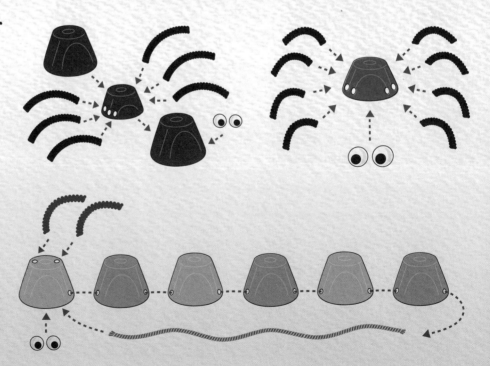

PIRATE SHIP!

I SAIL THE **SEVEN SEAS** WITH A DECK FULL OF **PIRATES**, STOPPING OFF AT **DESERT ISLANDS** IN SEARCH OF BURIED **TREASURE**.

AAARRRRRR!

YOU WILL NEED

- ONE LARGE EGG CARTON (FOR 12 EGGS)
- YELLOW AND BROWN PAINT
- SAFETY SCISSORS
- RED PAPER
- CRAFT STICKS
- TAPE
- BLACK CARDSTOCK
- STRING OR COTTON THREAD
- COLORFUL PAPER
- BLACK OR WHITE PAPER

DID YOU KNOW?

PIRATES WERE SUPERSTITIOUS AND THOUGHT THAT WHISTLING ON A SHIP WOULD BRING ON STORMS.

SET THE SCENE

Tear strips of yellow, orange, and white paper (you can use old magazines if you want!) and glue them to a piece of blue paper to make a collage island in the middle of the seven seas. Now turn the page to make your pirate ship.

STORMY WEATHER WON'T GET IN THE WAY OF ME AND MY QUEST FOR TREASURE, OH NO!

GO FURTHER!

MAKE A WHOLE FLEET OF MINI BATTLESHIPS USING EGG CARTON CUPS. TURN OVER TO FIND OUT HOW!

I'M A PIRATE SHIP!

1

Carefully cut the lid away from your egg carton, then paint the outside brown and the inside yellow. Let this dry.

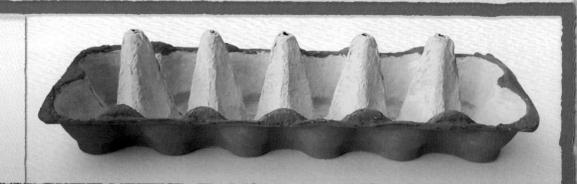

2

To make a sail, cut out a paper rectangle (around 6 in by 4-1/2 in). Snip a slit in the top and bottom of the flag to thread the craft stick through. Make two sails and tape them to your ship.

3

Cut out an anchor shape from black cardstock and tape a length of string or cotton thread to the top. Tape the other end to your ship.

4

Make bunting by cutting small triangles from colorful paper. Fold each triangle over some string or cotton thread and tape in place.

5

Give your ship an extra pirate touch by making a Jolly Roger flag. Ahoy, me hearties!

I AM NOT AN EGG CARTON...

I'M A BATTLESHIP!

To make a fleet of mini ships, cut out the cups from your egg carton and paint them brown. Wrap rectangles of white paper around toothpicks to make the sails, and a diamond of black paper to make a pirate flag (don't forget the skull and crossbones!). Add a ball of modeling clay to your boat and attach your toothpick sails.

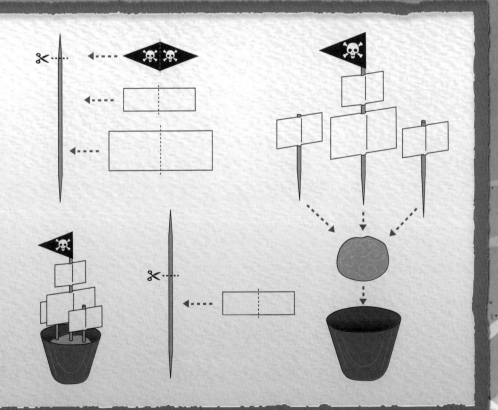

DRAGON!

I AM A **FIRE-BREATHING DRAGON**, NOT JUST SOME OLD EGG CARTON.

I LOVE TO **SOAR** HIGH UP IN THE **CLOUDS** AND **ALL OVER** THE LAND.

ROAR!

YOU WILL NEED

- ONE LARGE EGG CARTON (FOR 12 EGGS)
- GREEN PAINT
- BLACK PEN OR PAINT
- TWO BOTTLE TOPS
- WHITE PAPER
- SAFETY SCISSORS
- GLUE AND TAPE
- YELLOW AND WHITE PAPER
- TISSUE PAPER
- TAPE

SET THE SCENE

Make a fairy-tale setting full of forests and mountains by attaching different shades of green paper on top of each other and painting some trees. On the next page you can make your own dragon to soar over the landscape. What are you waiting for?

WITH MY **FANGS** AND **SPIKES**, IT CAN BE HARD TO MAKE **FRIENDS!**

ROAR!

GO FURTHER!

DON'T STOP THERE... YOU CAN MAKE A SLITHERING SNAKE WITH A FORKED TONGUE ON THE NEXT PAGE.

I'M A DRAGON!

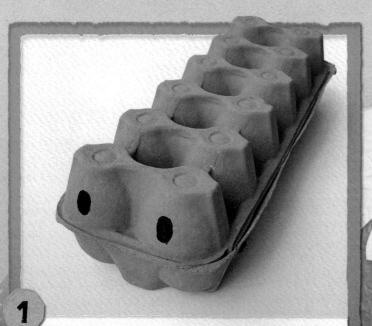

1

Paint your egg carton green all over and let it dry. Then paint or draw some black nostrils.

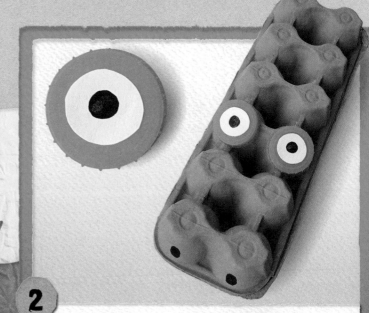

2

For the eyes, cut out two white circles and attach them to green bottle tops. Paint or draw some black pupils, then attach these to your dragon.

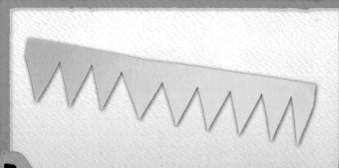

3

Next, cut a strip of zigzags out of a piece of yellow paper. It should be long enough to reach down the dragon's back. Tape it in place.

4

Cut two dragon wings out of yellow paper. Draw lines on your wings like this, then tape them to either side of your dragon.

5

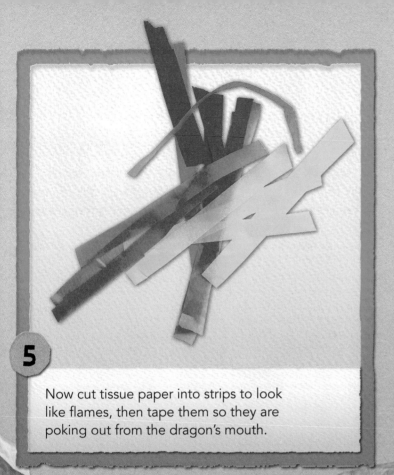

Now cut tissue paper into strips to look like flames, then tape them so they are poking out from the dragon's mouth.

6

For the fangs, cut two triangles from white paper or cardstock and glue them in place.

I AM NOT AN EGG CARTON...

I AM A SLIPPERY SNAKE!

Cut the egg cups out of a large egg carton and paint them your favorite snaky colors. Use a pencil to carefully make a hole in the top of each cup, then thread a piece of string through. Finish your snake with a forked tongue and googly eyes!

MUSIC SHAKERS!

WE'RE A BAND OF
MERRY MUSIC MAKERS.
GIVE US A RATTLE AND
MAKE A SWEET BEAT.

WE ARE PACKED
WITH DRIED BEANS,
AND WE CREATE THE
MUSIC OF DREAMS.

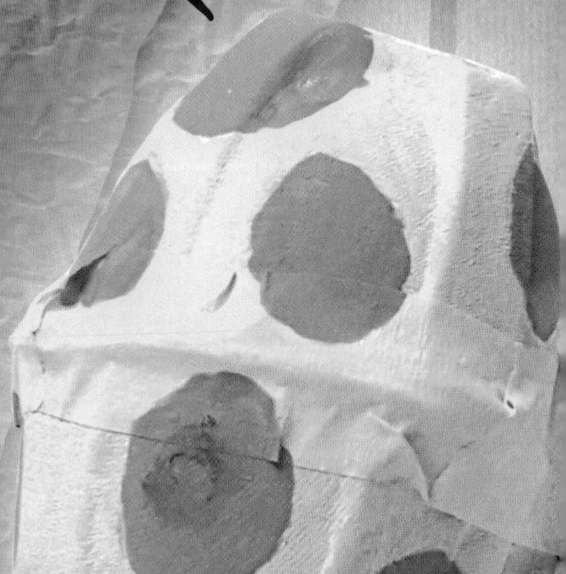

SHAKE!

YOU WILL NEED
- ONE EGG CARTON
- SAFETY SCISSORS
- UNCOOKED RICE
- TAPE
- PAINTS
- PAINTBRUSHES

SET THE SCENE

Make a stage suitable for a rockstar! Use a brown cardstock base and add blue or red strips as the curtain. Sprinkle with glitter for added sparkle! Now turn the page to make your own music band!

DID YOU KNOW?

SHAKERS LIKE THESE ARE PART OF THE PERCUSSION FAMILY OF INSTRUMENTS.

RATTLE!

ROLL!

GO FURTHER!

COOL DOWN AFTER ALL THAT MUSIC MAKING WITH A CARTON OF DELICIOUS ICE-CREAM CONES! TURN THE PAGE TO FIND OUT HOW.

1

Carefully cut two egg cups out of your egg carton.

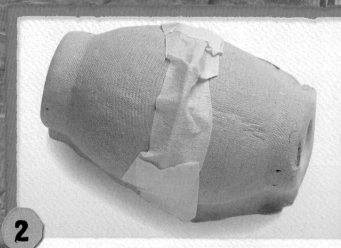

2

Fill one egg cup with uncooked rice and tape the second egg cup to the top like a lid. Make sure the tape completely seals any gaps.

3

Draw some patterns on your shaker before adding color with your paints. We chose spots, stripes, and star prints.

4

Let your shaker dry completely and get ready to make some music!

5

To complete your brilliant band, try switching the ingredients inside to see what different sounds you can make. Try these ideas:

- raw lentils
- uncooked pasta
- dried beans
- rice
- corn kernels

I AM NOT AN EGG CARTON...

I'M AN ICE-CREAM PARLOR!

Cut the central dividers out of the bottom of an egg carton. Flip them upside down to make your ice-cream cone shape. Use pompoms for the ice cream and small beads for the sprinkles. Then use another egg carton to stand your ice cream cones in.

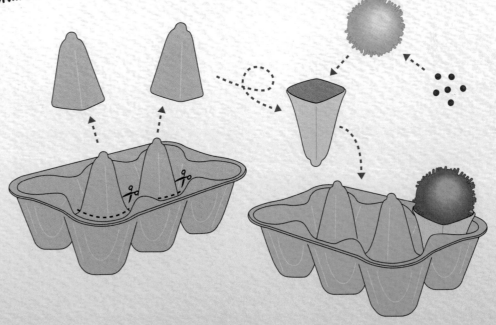

OCTOPUS!

I LIVE ON THE BOTTOM OF **THE OCEAN**, NOT THE BOTTOM OF THE **LAUNDRY BASKET!**

YOU WILL NEED

- ONE COLORFUL SOCK
- COTTON BATTING
- SAFETY SCISSORS
- GLUE
- GOOGLY EYES

LET'S GO FOR A DIP!

SET THE SCENE

Paint blue and green waves on a piece of cardstock until there is no white remaining, then fill it with cut-out fish and exciting sea creatures. You could use aluminum foil to make super shiny fish and attach little stones or shells to make a seafloor. Your octopus friends will feel right at home in this watery world.

DID YOU KNOW?
OCTOPUSES HAVE NO BONES, BUT THEY DO HAVE 3 HEARTS AND 9 BRAINS!

WITH MY **8 LEGS** AND **COLORFUL** PATTERNS, THERE ARE **NO OTHER** ANIMALS ON THE **PLANET** LIKE ME.

GO FURTHER!

WANT TO TRY SOMETHING A LITTLE DIFFERENT? TURN THE PAGE TO MAKE THESE FUNNY FACES.

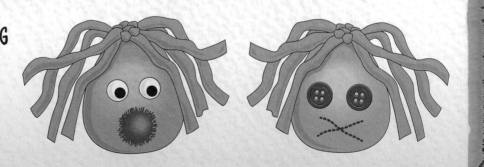

I'M AN OCTOPUS!

1

Push a handful of cotton batting to the toe end of your sock to make the body. It should fill up to halfway down your sock.

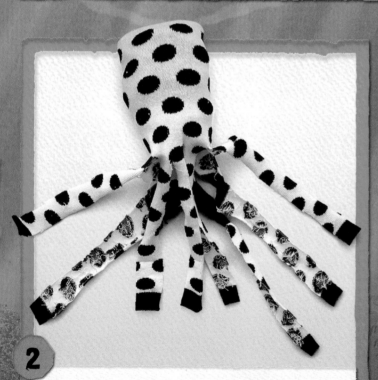

2

Carefully cut eight strips. Start at the open end of your sock and cut until you have almost reached the stuffing.

3

Hold a leg and tie it in a knot with the leg that is opposite it. Keep doing this until your octopus stuffing is sealed.

4

Trim the ends of your legs to make points then attach some googly eyes.

5

Now you can make lots of octopus pals in different colors!

I AM NOT A SOCK...

I'M A FAB FUNNY FACE!

Have fun making these little chaps. Just follow Steps 1-3, then turn your stuffed sock upside down so that the legs become hair. Add some googly eyes, then use a button or a small pompom for the nose. Stitch or glue some cotton batting at the bottom to make a smiley mouth. Who will you create?

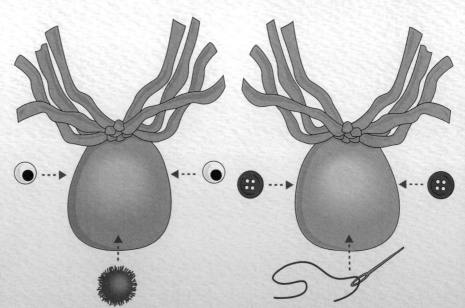

DOG TOY!

I'M A DOG TOY READY TO PLAY, AND TUG OF WAR IS MY FAVORITE GAME OF ALL.

LET'S PLAY.

DID YOU KNOW? DOGS CAN SMELL UP TO 10,000 TIMES BETTER THAN HUMANS CAN.

YOU WILL NEED
- THREE SOCKS IN DIFFERENT COLORS

YOU CAN **GIVE ME** TO YOUR DOG AS A **SPECIAL** TREAT WHEN IT'S BEEN **EXTRA GOOD.**

WOOF! WOOF!

GO FURTHER!

IF YOU HAVE AN EXTRA SOCK, YOU CAN USE THE SAME TECHNIQUE TO MAKE ANOTHER TOY. TURN THE PAGE TO FIND OUT HOW!

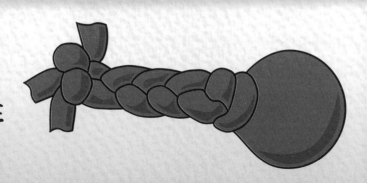

I AM NOT A SOCK...
I'M A DOG TOY!

1 Tie all three socks together at the opening by making a knot as shown.

2 Now, start to braid the socks together by bringing the right sock into the middle, then the left sock into the middle.

3 Keep going until you reach near the bottom, but leave enough space to tie another knot.

4

Finally, tie a knot on this end of your braid to hold it together.

I AM NOT A SOCK...

I'M ANOTHER DOG TOY!

To make a different type of dog toy, put a dog ball into the end of the sock. Tie a big knot to hold it in place, then cut the leftover sock into three strands. Braid these strands and tie another knot on the end, and your dog chew is ready! This makes a great toy for playing fetch with, too.

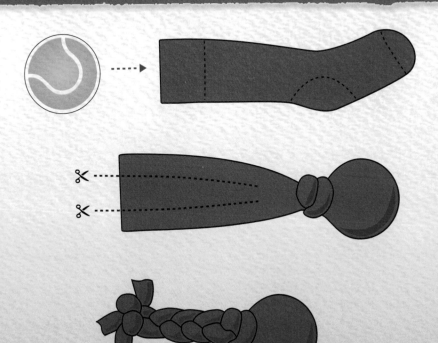

SNOWMAN!

BEING **FROSTY** AND **ICE-COLD** IS MY **FAVORITE** WAY TO BE, BECAUSE I AM A **SNOWMAN!**

DID YOU KNOW? JAPAN IS THE SNOWIEST PLACE IN THE WORLD.

BRRRR!

BRRRR!

YOU WILL NEED

- ONE WHITE SOCK
- COTTON BATTING
- ONE COLORFUL SOCK
- THREAD
- BUTTONS
- BLACK PEN
- ORANGE PAPER
- GLUE
- SAFETY SCISSORS

I LOVE TO **DRESS UP** IN A BIG **BOBBLE HAT** AND **SCARF**. JUST CHECK OUT MY **COAL EYES** AND **CARROT** NOSE!

SET THE SCENE

Make a frosty background scene for your snowman to stand in. Use cotton batting for snow and bits of aluminum foil for slippery ice. Glue them to a piece of blue cardstock. Try drawing more snowmen in the picture to keep your snow sock buddy company!

I'M THE SNOWMAN THAT NEVER MELTS!

GO FURTHER!

LET'S MAKE A SOCK PENGUIN TO ADD TO YOUR SNOWY SCENE, TOO. WE'LL SHOW YOU HOW ON THE NEXT PAGE.

I AM NOT A SOCK...
I'M A SNOWMAN!

1

Push cotton batting into a white sock. Leave enough space so that you can tie a knot at the end.

2

Trim around the knot to neaten it up. Now, make a scarf from a strip of colorful sock and tie it to make a head and body.

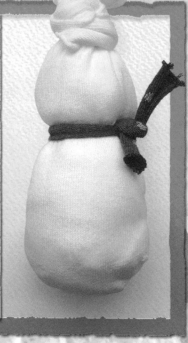

3

Take the rest of the colorful sock and cut the ankle part away like this. Pinch it into a hat shape and tie some thread around it to keep it in place.

4

Now that your hat's on, it's time to glue some bright red buttons to the snowman's tummy.

5

Draw two eyes and a dotted grin using a black pen.

6

Cut a carrot nose out of orange paper and glue it on your snowman's face.

I AM NOT A SOCK...

I'M A PENGUIN!

Stuff a black sock so that it's around ¾ full and tie a knot on the top. Next, tie a piece of thread around the penguin to make a head and body shape. Cut out round pieces of white fabric (you could use a piece of a white sock) and glue this on to make the penguin's tummy and face. Add googly eyes, tape on a yellow paper beak, and make a hat and scarf from a colorful sock.

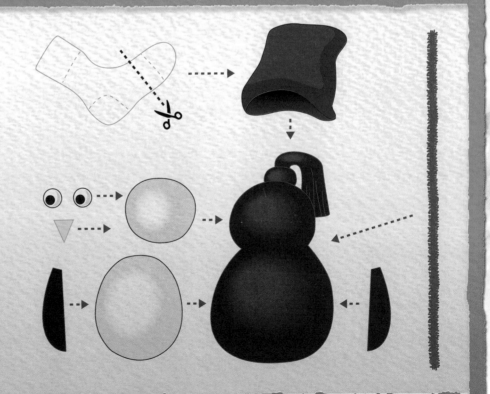

RABBIT! HOP TO IT...

I HOP ALL OVER THE GARDEN, AND I STRETCH UP TALL TO GET A GOOD VIEW OF EVERYTHING.

YOU WILL NEED

- ONE SOCK
- TAPE
- UNCOOKED RICE
- THREAD
- SAFETY SCISSORS
- ABSORBENT COTTON
- GOOGLY EYES
- GLUE
- RIBBON

SET THE SCENE

Cut some tasty veggies out of colorful paper for your bunny to munch on. Try orange carrots, or some green cabbage and lettuce. Lay them in a cardboard box to create a whole vegetable patch!

HAVE YOU SEEN MY CUTE **BOB TAIL** AND **BIG FLOPPY** EARS?

IF YOU BRING ME A **CARROT**, I'LL BE YOUR PAL FOR LIFE.

GO FURTHER!

ONCE YOU'VE MADE ONE RABBIT, WHY NOT USE DIFFERENT-SIZED SOCKS TO MAKE A WHOLE BUNNY FAMILY?

DID YOU KNOW?

WHEN RABBITS ARE HAPPY, THEY JUMP INTO THE AIR AND SPIN AROUND.

I AM NOT A SOCK...
I AM A RABBIT!

1

Stretch the end of your sock over a roll of sticky tape like this. This makes it easier to fill your sock with uncooked rice.

2

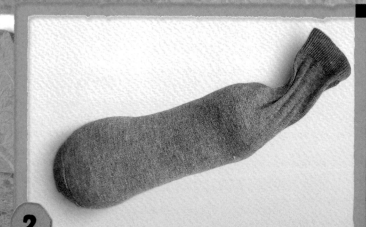

Fill your sock with rice until it is roughly ¾ full. Take out the tape, then tie the top of the sock tightly with some yarn or thread.

3

Then use more thread to make a separate head and body shape like this. Make sure that the rabbit's head is a little bit smaller than the body.

4

To make the ears, snip the ankle part of the sock in half. Then trim to make each end pointed.

5

Make a fluffy bob tail from a ball of absorbent cotton and glue it to the back of your bunny.

6

Stick on googly eyes and stitch a cross to make a mouth. Finish with a sweet ribbon.

I AM NOT A SOCK...

I'M A WHOLE RABBIT FAMILY!

Find different sized socks to make a whole family of rabbits! Use little socks to make some adorable baby bunnies. What will you name them all?

DINOSAURRRR!

I'M A GREAT BIG **DINO**, CAN'T YOU SEE? I'M FAR TOO **FiERCE** TO BE A CEREAL BOX. YOU WILL KNOW IT'S ME WHEN I OPEN MY HUGE JAW AND **ROAR, ROAR, ROAR!**

YOU WILL NEED

- ONE CEREAL BOX
- SAFETY SCISSORS
- CARD
- GLUE
- PAINTS
- WHITE CARD
- YELLOW CARD

SET THE SCENE

Create a whole land for your dino to explore! Scrunch up magazines or newspapers to make big boulders and rocks for your prehistoric pal to stomp through. You could cut out big dino footprints from paper and place them around your room. Make your own tooth-tastic dino hat to bring this cereal box to life. Flip the page to find out how!

DID YOU KNOW? DINOSAURS ROAMED THE PLANET FOR 165 MILLION YEARS IN THE MESOZOIC ERA.

ROOAAAAR!

GO FURTHER!

DO YOU LOVE HORSES? WELL, YOU CAN MAKE ONE OF THOSE TOO! TURN THE PAGE TO FOLLOW OUR EASY STEP-BY-STEP GUIDE.

I'M A DINOSAUR!

1

Carefully cut a hole out of the front of your cereal box. It will need to be big enough to fit the top of your head comfortably. Turn the cereal box over so the hole is underneath.

2

Cut two eye shapes like this out of cardstock and tape these to your cereal box. Paint your box green and let it dry.

3

Make some beady eyes by painting big black dots on white circles of paper. Attach these to your dino, then glue triangles cut out of white card to make pointed teeth.

4

Next, paint two black nostrils. You can also finger-paint yellow splotches all over your dino to look like scales! Let them dry.

5

Cut out a strip of zigzags from yellow paper.

6

Tape the zigzag strip so that it sits in the middle of your dino's eyes like this, and you're all done! Place your new pal on top of your head and transform into a roaring dinosaur!

I AM NOT A CEREAL BOX...
I'M A HORSE'S HEAD!

To make a horse's head, just turn the box on its side and cut out a mouth as shown. Attach a red tongue and add two ears and eyes. Finally, give your horse a mane made of cotton batting.

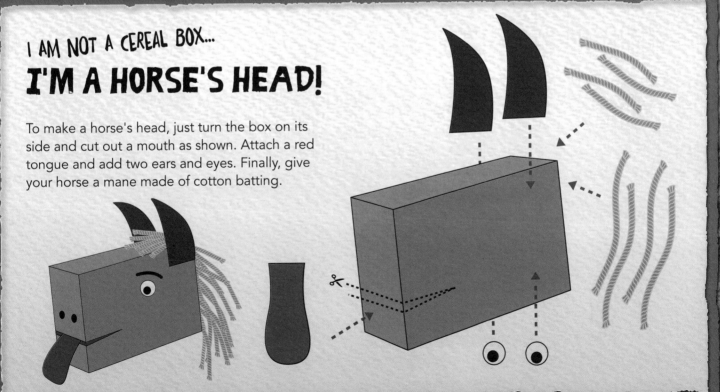

ROCK GUITAR!

LET'S RAISE THE ROOF! I AM A ROCK STAR GUITAR THAT ALWAYS PUTS ON A SHOW. TUNE IN YOUR EARS BECAUSE I'M READY FOR MY BIG SOLO!

YOU WILL NEED

- ONE CEREAL BOX
- SAFETY SCISSORS
- PAINT
- LONG CARDBOARD TUBE
- PIPE CLEANERS
- TAPE
- WOOL
- GLUE
- CARDSTOCK
- COLORFUL PAPER TO DECORATE

SET THE SCENE

Make stage lights for your music show! Paint some empty, clean yogurt pots and when they're dry, tape different colors of bright tissue paper over the ends of them. You could tape a few pots together to make a row of disco lights. Make a cereal box's dreams of fame come true and turn it into a rock star guitar. Our step-by-step guide is on the next page.

TWANG TWAAANG!

DID YOU KNOW?
GUITARS USUALLY HAVE SIX STRINGS, BUT 4-STRING AND 12-STRING VERSIONS ARE POPULAR TOO! YOU CAN EVEN FIND 7, 8, 9, AND 10-STRING VERSIONS.

GO FURTHER!

COMPLETE YOUR BAND BY MAKING A DRUM SO YOUR FRIENDS CAN JOIN IN WITH YOU! TURN THE PAGE AND WE'LL SHOW YOU HOW.

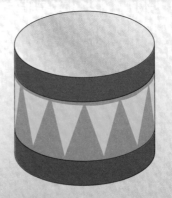

I AM NOT A CEREAL BOX...

I'M A ROCK GUITAR!

1

Carefully cut a circle out of the front of your cereal box. Then choose a bright color to paint it and let it dry.

2

Next, paint your cardboard tube in a different color. When dry, cut some pipe cleaners to 1-1/2 inches and tape them to the end.

3

Tuck the lid of the cereal box down to make a space, then push your long tube through. Tape it in place as shown.

4

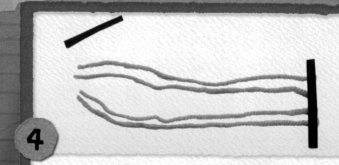

Use cotton string or yarn to make guitar strings. Make the yarn long enough to reach across the cereal box. Tape the ends of the yarn to a piece of black cardstock like this.

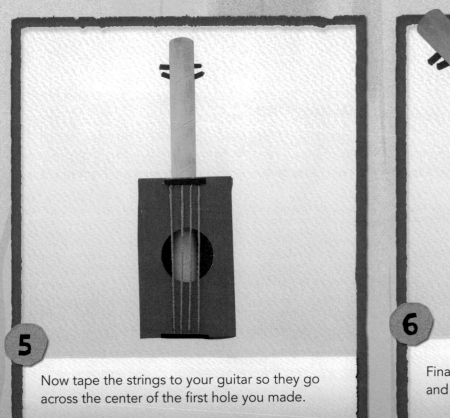

5

Now tape the strings to your guitar so they go across the center of the first hole you made.

6

Finally, decorate your guitar with a fun design and get ready to rock out!

I AM NOT A CEREAL BOX...
I'M A DRUM!

Did you know it's easy to turn a rectangular cereal box into a round drum? Use the instructions here to draw a plan on a flattened box. Cut all the pieces out and attach them together with tape as shown. Stick a couple of corks on the end of drinking straws to make drumsticks.

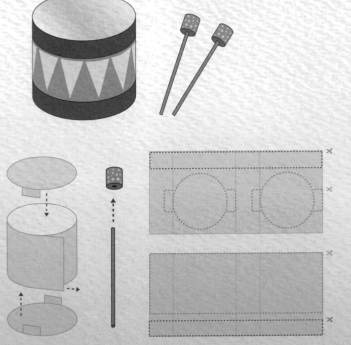

ROBOT!

I AM A ROBOT, AND BEING SMART IS MY MIDDLE NAME! I'M MADE FROM THE VERY BEST TECHNOLOGY AROUND, NOT JUST SOME SILLY OLD CARDBOARD BOX!

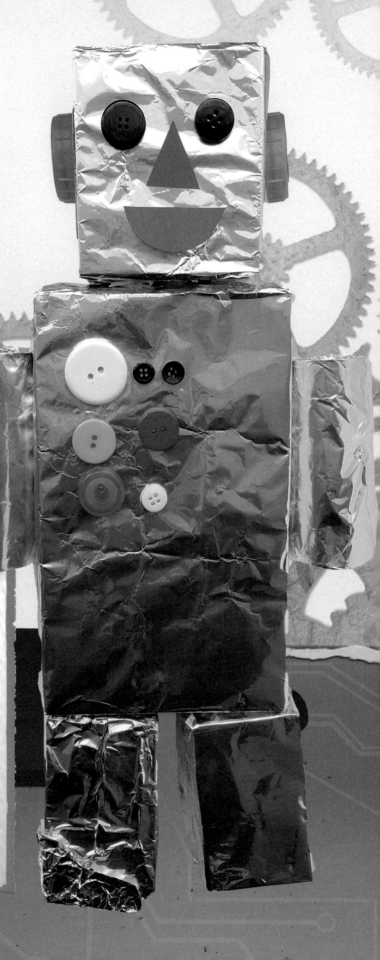

YOU WILL NEED

- ONE BIG CEREAL BOX
- THREE MINI CEREAL BOXES
- ALUMINUM FOIL
- TAPE
- CARDBOARD TUBES
- TAPE
- BUTTONS AND BOTTLE TOPS
- GLUE
- COLORFUL PAPER
- SAFETY SCISSORS

SET THE SCENE

Make your robot feel at home by creating a techno-fabulous background for it to stand in. Draw cogs, wheels, and buttons on a big piece of cardstock and use pencils, pens, or gray paint to fill them in. Use bits of aluminum foil to build up texture and add extra shine. Turn the page to find out how to make your own nifty robot buddy.

DID YOU KNOW? LEONARDO DA VINCI CAME UP WITH PLANS FOR A ROBOT IN THE LATE 1400s!

DO THE ROBOT DANCE!

GO FURTHER!

IF A WHOLE ROBOT IS A BIT TOO MUCH FOR YOU, WHY NOT MAKE A GIANT ROBOT HEAD INSTEAD? JUST TURN THE PAGE TO FIND OUT HOW.

I'M A ROBOT!

1

Cover your big and small cereal boxes in aluminum foil, then tape the small box on top of the big box to make a robot head and body.

2

For the arms, cover two toilet paper or paper towel roll in aluminum foil and tape them to each side of the body like this. If you don't have spare tubes, you could make your own by rolling pieces of cardboard and taping in place.

3

For the legs, cover two more small cereal boxes in foil. Turn them on their sides and tape them to the bottom of your robot.

4

Glue bottle tops on each side of the head for ears, then attach buttons for eyes.

5

Cut a triangle and semicircle out of red paper to make a nose and a mouth for your robot. Attach these to make a friendly face.

6

Finally, give your robot lots of dials and knobs using spare buttons and bottle tops. You could even give him a different mouth. Get creating!

I AM NOT A CEREAL BOX...
I'M A GIANT ROBOT HEAD!

To make your huge robot face, turn your large cereal box on its side and cover it in colorful paper or aluminum foil. Draw around a cup on colorful paper to make two large eyes, then make triangle nose and rectangle mouth shapes. Use white paper or stickers for the teeth and cut up bits of the toilet paper roll for the ears, too!

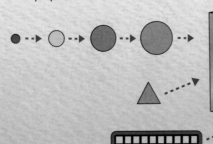

MARBLE RUN!

WOULD YOU LIKE TO RACE? I AM A **MARVELOUS** MARBLE RUN FULL OF **SLOPES AND RAMPS** TO RACE FROM THE TOP ALL THE WAY DOWN.

READY, SET... **GO!**

YOU WILL NEED

- ONE CEREAL BOX
- PAINTS
- PAINTBRUSHES
- SAFETY SCISSORS
- TAPE

SET THE SCENE

Why not turn your marble run into a fairground stall? Make signs saying "Have a try!" and "Marvelous marble run!" and then set up your stall on a small table. Now, turn the page to discover how to make your fun-tastic marble run.

GO FURTHER!

YOU CAN ALSO MAKE A MEGA MAZE FOR YOUR MARBLES TO ZOOM AROUND. TURN THE PAGE AND ALL WILL BE REVEALED!

DID YOU KNOW?
THE LONGEST MARBLE RUN MEASURES 1.75 MILES!

ROLL WITH IT!

I AM NOT A CEREAL BOX...

I'M A MARBLE RUN!

1

Carefully cut off the front of your cereal box so it looks like this. Keep the leftover cardboard safe as you will need it in Step 3.

2

Paint the inside of your marble run with bright paints and let it dry.

3

To make the paths for your marbles to roll down, cut your leftover cardboard into four strips. Paint them in bright colors and let them dry.

4

Fold the end of each strip of cardboard like this.

5 Use the fold to tape each strip to the inside of your cereal box to make a sloped path. Tape each path on alternate sides and keep going until the path leads all the way to the bottom.

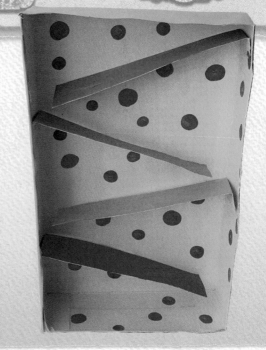

6 Now decorate your marble run by finger painting colorful polka dots on the background.

I AM NOT A CEREAL BOX...

I'M A MARBLE MAZE!

To make an awesome maze, cut around the sides of a cereal box, then lay one half down flat. Build a maze path using strips of colorful cardboard and tape them in place. You can make your maze as challenging as you want by creating dead ends and lots of twists and turns. To play, gently tip your maze from side to side.

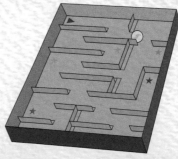

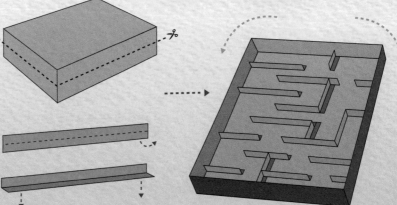

YOUR DESIGNS

NOW iT'S OVER TO YOU... THE ONLY THiNG HOLDiNG YOUR EMPTY TOiLET PAPER ROLLS, EGG CARTONS, CEREAL BOXES, AND OLD SOCKS BACK FROM GREATNESS iS YOUR OWN iMAGiNATiON! SKETCH YOUR iDEAS HERE—WE'VE GIVEN YOU A FEW OUTLINES TO GET YOU STARTED.

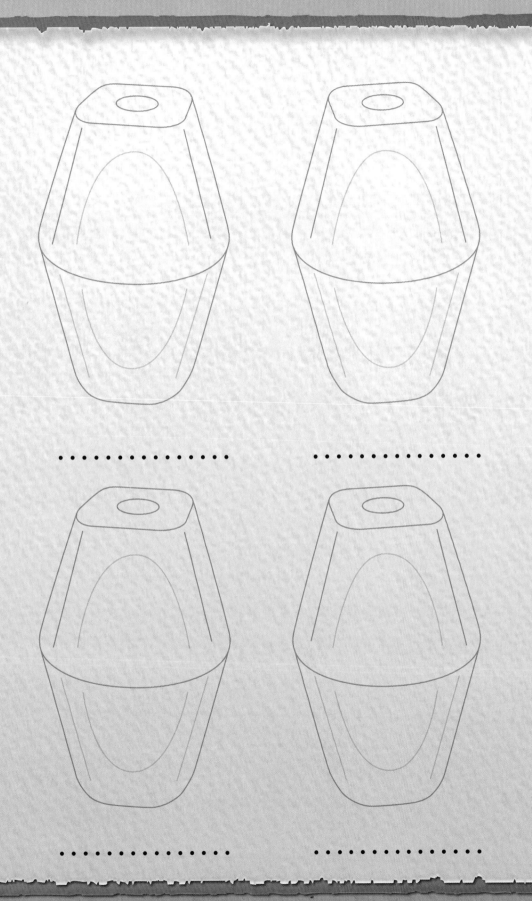

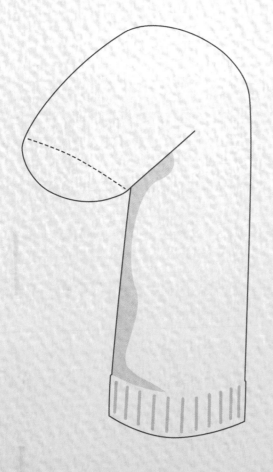
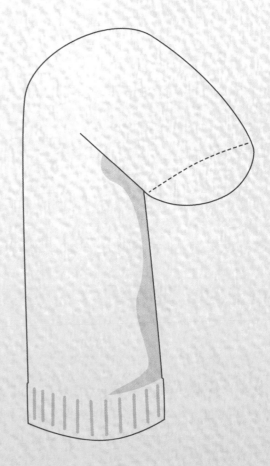

· · · · · · · · · · · · · · ·   · · · · · · · · · · · · · · ·

DON'T FORGET TO GIVE YOUR CREATIONS A GOOD NAME...
THE LOCH NESS SOCKMONSTER, PERHAPS? WHATEVER YOU
CHOOSE IS SURE TO BE A SOCKCESS.

. . . .

. . . .

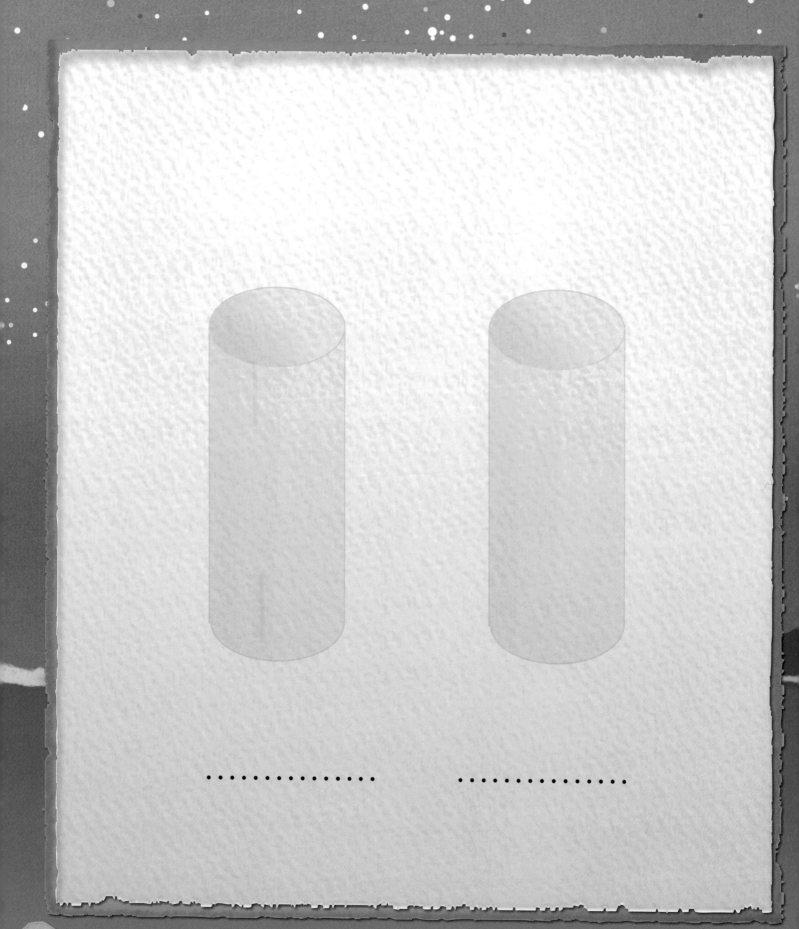

shark fins

shark fins

googly eyes

bat wings

castle door

unicorn ear

unicorn horn

unicorn ear

mermaid's tail

pirate hat

candy cane

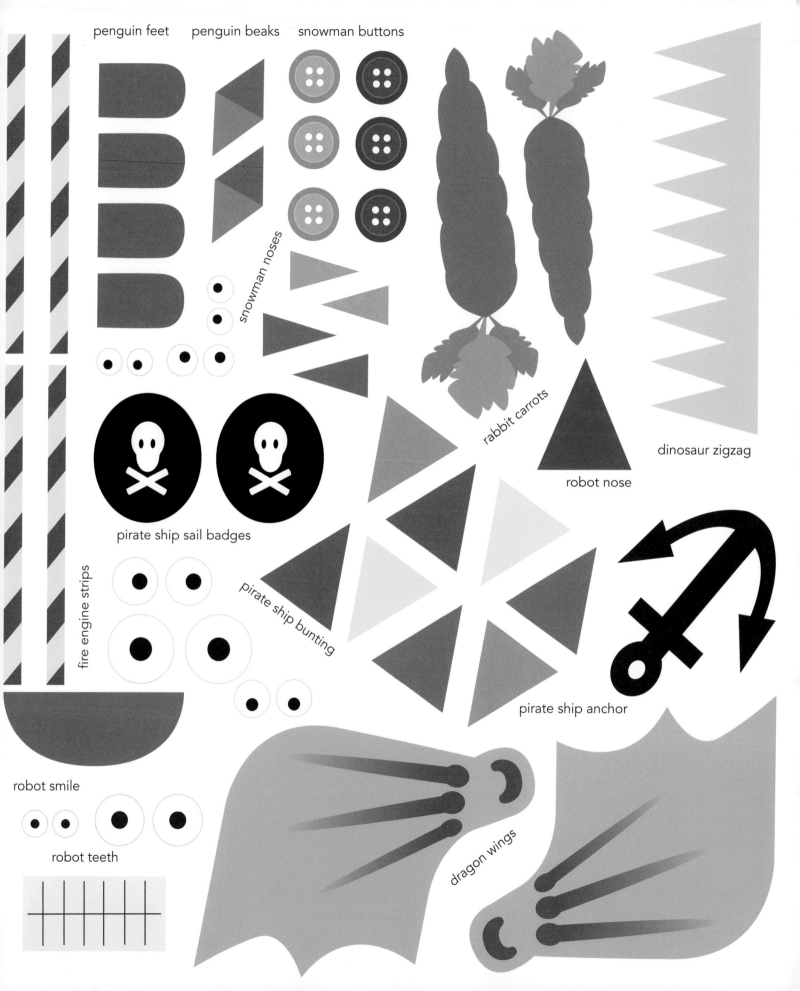

penguin feet

penguin beaks

snowman buttons

snowman noses

rabbit carrots

dinosaur zigzag

robot nose

pirate ship sail badges

fire engine strips

pirate ship bunting

pirate ship anchor

robot smile

robot teeth

dragon wings